This Planner Belongs To :

_____

good things take time

2019 Calendar

July

S	M	T	W	T	F	S
30	1	2	3	4	5	6
7	8	9	10	11	12	13
14	15	16	17	18	19	20
21	22	23	24	25	26	27
28	29	30	31	1	2	3
4	5	6	7	8	9	10

August

S	M	T	W	T	F	S
28	29	30	31	1	2	3
4	5	6	7	8	9	10
11	12	13	14	15	16	17
18	19	20	21	22	23	24
25	26	27	28	29	30	31
1	2	3	4	5	6	7

September

S	M	T	W	T	F	S
1	2	3	4	5	6	7
8	9	10	11	12	13	14
15	16	17	18	19	20	21
22	23	24	25	26	27	28
29	30	1	2	3	4	5
6	7	8	9	10	11	12

October

S	M	T	W	T	F	S
29	30	1	2	3	4	5
6	7	8	9	10	11	12
13	14	15	16	17	18	19
20	21	22	23	24	25	26
27	28	29	30	31	1	2
3	4	5	6	7	8	9

November

S	M	T	W	T	F	S
27	28	29	30	31	1	2
3	4	5	6	7	8	9
10	11	12	13	14	15	16
17	18	19	20	21	22	23
24	25	26	27	28	29	30
1	2	3	4	5	6	7

December

S	M	T	W	T	F	S
1	2	3	4	5	6	7
8	9	10	11	12	13	14
15	16	17	18	19	20	21
22	23	24	25	26	27	28
29	30	31	1	2	3	4
5	6	7	8	9	10	11

Note

2020 Calendar

January

S	M	T	W	T	F	S
29	30	31	1	2	3	4
5	6	7	8	9	10	11
12	13	14	15	16	17	18
19	20	21	22	23	24	25
26	27	28	29	30	31	1
2	3	4	5	6	7	8

February

S	M	T	W	T	F	S
26	27	28	29	30	31	1
2	3	4	5	6	7	8
9	10	11	12	13	14	15
16	17	18	19	20	21	22
23	24	25	26	27	28	29
1	2	3	4	5	6	7

March

S	M	T	W	T	F	S
1	2	3	4	5	6	7
8	9	10	11	12	13	14
15	16	17	18	19	20	21
22	23	24	25	26	27	28
29	30	31	1	2	3	4
5	6	7	8	9	10	11

April

S	M	T	W	T	F	S
29	30	31	1	2	3	4
5	6	7	8	9	10	11
12	13	14	15	16	17	18
19	20	21	22	23	24	25
26	27	28	29	30	1	2
3	4	5	6	7	8	9

May

S	M	T	W	T	F	S
26	27	28	29	30	1	2
3	4	5	6	7	8	9
10	11	12	13	14	15	16
17	18	19	20	21	22	23
24	25	26	27	28	29	30
31	1	2	3	4	5	6

June

S	M	T	W	T	F	S
31	1	2	3	4	5	6
7	8	9	10	11	12	13
14	15	16	17	18	19	20
21	22	23	24	25	26	27
28	29	30	1	2	3	4
5	6	7	8	9	10	11

Note

2020 Calendar

July

S	M	T	W	T	F	S
28	29	30	1	2	3	4
5	6	7	8	9	10	11
12	13	14	15	16	17	18
19	20	21	22	23	24	25
26	27	28	29	30	31	1
2	3	4	5	6	7	8

August

S	M	T	W	T	F	S
26	27	28	29	30	31	1
2	3	4	5	6	7	8
9	10	11	12	13	14	15
16	17	18	19	20	21	22
23	24	25	26	27	28	29
30	31	1	2	3	4	5

September

S	M	T	W	T	F	S
30	31	1	2	3	4	5
6	7	8	9	10	11	12
13	14	15	16	17	18	19
20	21	22	23	24	25	26
27	28	29	30	1	2	3
4	5	6	7	8	9	10

October

S	M	T	W	T	F	S
27	28	29	30	1	2	3
4	5	6	7	8	9	10
11	12	13	14	15	16	17
18	19	20	21	22	23	24
25	26	27	28	29	30	31
1	2	3	4	5	6	7

November

S	M	T	W	T	F	S
1	2	3	4	5	6	7
8	9	10	11	12	13	14
15	16	17	18	19	20	21
22	23	24	25	26	27	28
29	30	1	2	3	4	5
6	7	8	9	10	11	12

December

S	M	T	W	T	F	S
29	30	1	2	3	4	5
6	7	8	9	10	11	12
13	14	15	16	17	18	19
20	21	22	23	24	25	26
27	28	29	30	31	1	2
3	4	5	6	7	8	9

Note

Yearly Summary

Summary	Budgeted	Actual
Income		
Bill Expenses		
Other Expenses		
Savings		
Total		

July	
Income	
Bill Expenses	
Other Expenses	
Savings	
Total	

August	
Income	
Bill Expenses	
Other Expenses	
Savings	
Total	

September	
Income	
Bill Expenses	
Other Expenses	
Savings	
Total	

October	
Income	
Bill Expenses	
Other Expenses	
Savings	
Total	

November	
Income	
Bill Expenses	
Other Expenses	
Savings	
Total	

December	
Income	
Bill Expenses	
Other Expenses	
Savings	
Total	

Note

Yearly Summary

Summary	Budgeted	Actual
Income		
Bill Expenses		
Other Expenses		
Savings		
Total		

January	
Income	
Bill Expenses	
Other Expenses	
Savings	
Total	

February	
Income	
Bill Expenses	
Other Expenses	
Savings	
Total	

March	
Income	
Bill Expenses	
Other Expenses	
Savings	
Total	

April	
Income	
Bill Expenses	
Other Expenses	
Savings	
Total	

May	
Income	
Bill Expenses	
Other Expenses	
Savings	
Total	

June	
Income	
Bill Expenses	
Other Expenses	
Savings	
Total	

July	
Income	
Bill Expenses	
Other Expenses	
Savings	
Total	

August	
Income	
Bill Expenses	
Other Expenses	
Savings	
Total	

September	
Income	
Bill Expenses	
Other Expenses	
Savings	
Total	

October	
Income	
Bill Expenses	
Other Expenses	
Savings	
Total	

November	
Income	
Bill Expenses	
Other Expenses	
Savings	
Total	

December	
Income	
Bill Expenses	
Other Expenses	
Savings	
Total	

Note

July 2019

Sunday	Monday	Tuesday	Wednesday
30	1	2	3
7	8	9	10
14	15	16	17
21	22	23	24
28	29	30	31

Parents' Day

Thursday	Friday	Saturday
4 Independence Day	5	6
11	12	13
18	19	20
25	26	27
1	2	3

June 2019

Su	M	Tu	W	Th	F	Sa
						1
2	3	4	5	6	7	8
9	10	11	12	13	14	15
16	17	18	19	20	21	22
23	24	25	26	27	28	29
30						

August 2019

Su	M	Tu	W	Th	F	Sa
				1	2	3
4	5	6	7	8	9	10
11	12	13	14	15	16	17
18	19	20	21	22	23	24
25	26	27	28	29	30	31

Monthly Budget

Income		
Income 1		
Income 1		
Other Income		
Total Income		

Goal :

Budget :

Bill To Be Paid	Date Due	Amount	Paid	Note
			○	
			○	
			○	
			○	
			○	
			○	
			○	
			○	
			○	
			○	
			○	
			○	
			○	
			○	
			○	
			○	
			○	
			○	
			○	
			○	
			○	
			○	
			○	
Total				

Monthly Budget

Other Expenses	Date	Amount	Note
Total			

Total Income

Total Expenses

Difference

Notes

Weekly Expense Tracker

 MON   **JULY 1, 2019**

Description	Amount
Total	

 TUE   **JULY 2, 2019**

Description	Amount
Total	

 WED   **JULY 3, 2019**

Description	Amount
Total	

 THU   **JULY 4, 2019**

Description	Amount
Total	

 FRI   **JULY 5, 2019**

Description	Amount
Total	

 SAT   **JULY 6, 2019**

Description	Amount
Total	

$ SUN $ **JULY 7, 2019**

Description	Amount
Total	

Notes

Weekly Expense Tracker

MON JULY 8, 2019

Description	Amount
Total	

 TUE JULY 9, 2019

Description	Amount
Total	

WED JULY 10, 2019

Description	Amount
Total	

THU JULY 11, 2019

Description	Amount
Total	

FRI JULY 12, 2019

Description	Amount
Total	

SAT JULY 13, 2019

Description	Amount
Total	

SUN JULY 14, 2019

Description	Amount
Total	

Notes

Weekly Expense Tracker

 MON JULY 15, 2019

Description	Amount
Total	

 TUE JULY 16, 2019

Description	Amount
Total	

 WED JULY 17, 2019

Description	Amount
Total	

 THU JULY 18, 2019

Description	Amount
Total	

 FRI JULY 19, 2019

Description	Amount
Total	

 SAT JULY 20, 2019

Description	Amount
Total	

$ SUN $ JULY 21, 2019

Description	Amount
Total	

Notes

Weekly Expense Tracker

 MON JULY 22, 2019

Description	Amount
Total	

 TUE JULY 23, 2019

Description	Amount
Total	

WED JULY 24, 2019

Description	Amount
Total	

THU JULY 25, 2019

Description	Amount
Total	

FRI JULY 26, 2019

Description	Amount
Total	

SAT JULY 27, 2019

Description	Amount
Total	

SUN JULY 28, 2019

Description	Amount
Total	

Notes

Weekly Expense Tracker

 MON JULY 29, 2019

Description	Amount
Total	

 TUE JULY 30, 2019

Description	Amount
Total	

WED JULY 31, 2019

Description	Amount
Total	

 THU AUGUST 1, 2019

Description	Amount
Total	

 FRI AUGUST 2, 2019

Description	Amount
Total	

 SAT AUGUST 3, 2019

Description	Amount
Total	

SUN AUGUST 4, 2019

Description	Amount
Total	

Notes

Note

August 2019

Sunday	Monday	Tuesday	Wednesday
28	29	30	31
Parents' Day			
4	5	6	7
	Summer Bank Holiday (UK)		
11	12	13	14
18	19	20	21
	Aviation Day		
25	26	27	28
	Late Summer Bank Holiday (UK)		

Thursday	Friday	Saturday
1	2	3
8	9	10
15	16	17
22	23	24
29	30	31

July 2019

Su	M	Tu	W	Th	F	Sa
	1	2	3	4	5	6
7	8	9	10	11	12	13
14	15	16	17	18	19	20
21	22	23	24	25	26	27
28	29	30	31			

September 2019

Su	M	Tu	W	Th	F	Sa
1	2	3	4	5	6	7
8	9	10	11	12	13	14
15	16	17	18	19	20	21
22	23	24	25	26	27	28
29	30					

Monthly Budget

Income		
Income 1		
Income 1		
Other Income		
Total Income		

Goal :

Budget :

Bill To Be Paid	Date Due	Amount	Paid	Note
			○	
			○	
			○	
			○	
			○	
			○	
			○	
			○	
			○	
			○	
			○	
			○	
			○	
			○	
			○	
			○	
			○	
			○	
			○	
			○	
			○	
			○	
			○	
Total				

Monthly Budget

Other Expenses	Date	Amount	Note
Total			

Total Income

Total Expenses

Difference

Notes

Weekly Expense Tracker

 MON   AUGUST 5, 2019   **TUE**   AUGUST 6, 2019   **WED**   AUGUST 7, 2019

Description	Amount
Total	

Description	Amount
Total	

Description	Amount
Total	

 THU   AUGUST 8, 2019   **FRI**   AUGUST 9, 2019   **SAT**   AUGUST 10, 2019

Description	Amount
Total	

Description	Amount
Total	

Description	Amount
Total	

$ SUN $ AUGUST 11, 2019

Description	Amount
Total	

Notes

Weekly Expense Tracker

 MON AUGUST 12, 2019   **TUE** AUGUST 13, 2019   **WED** AUGUST 14, 2019

Description	Amount	Description	Amount	Description	Amount
Total		Total		Total	

 THU AUGUST 15, 2019   **FRI** AUGUST 16, 2019   **SAT** AUGUST 17, 2019

Description	Amount	Description	Amount	Description	Amount
Total		Total		Total	

SUN AUGUST 18, 2019

Description	Amount
Total	

Notes

Weekly Expense Tracker

 MON   AUGUST 19, 2019   **TUE**   AUGUST 20, 2019   **WED**   AUGUST 21, 2019

Description	Amount	Description	Amount	Description	Amount
Total		**Total**		**Total**	

 THU   AUGUST 22, 2019   **FRI**   AUGUST 23, 2019   **SAT**   AUGUST 24, 2019

Description	Amount	Description	Amount	Description	Amount
Total		**Total**		**Total**	

$ SUN $ AUGUST 25, 2019

Description	Amount
Total	

Notes

Weekly Expense Tracker

MON AUGUST 26, 2019

Description	Amount
Total	

TUE AUGUST 27, 2019

Description	Amount
Total	

WED AUGUST 28, 2019

Description	Amount
Total	

THU AUGUST 29, 2019

Description	Amount
Total	

FRI AUGUST 30, 2019

Description	Amount
Total	

SAT AUGUST 31, 2019

Description	Amount
Total	

SUN SEPTEMBER 1, 2019

Description	Amount
Total	

Notes

September 2019

Sunday	Monday	Tuesday	Wednesday
1	2 *Labor Day*	3	4
8 *Grandparents Day*	9	10	11 *Patriot Day*
15	16	17 *Constitution Day*	18
22	23 *Autumnal equinox*	24	25
29	30 *Rosh Hashanah*	1	2

August 2019

Su	M	Tu	W	Th	F	Sa
				1	2	3
4	5	6	7	8	9	10
11	12	13	14	15	16	17
18	19	20	21	22	23	24
25	26	27	28	29	30	31

Thursday	Friday	Saturday
5	6	7
12	13	14
19	20	21
26	27	28
3	4	5

October 2019

Su	M	Tu	W	Th	F	Sa
		1	2	3	4	5
6	7	8	9	10	11	12
13	14	15	16	17	18	19
20	21	22	23	24	25	26
27	28	29	30	31		

Monthly Budget

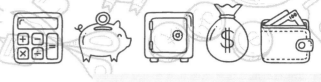

Income		
Income 1		
Income 1		
Other Income		
Total Income		

Goal :

Budget :

Bill To Be Paid	Date Due	Amount	Paid	Note
			○	
			○	
			○	
			○	
			○	
			○	
			○	
			○	
			○	
			○	
			○	
			○	
			○	
			○	
			○	
			○	
			○	
			○	
			○	
			○	
			○	
			○	
			○	
Total				

Monthly Budget

Other Expenses	Date	Amount	Note
Total			

Total Income

Total Expenses

Difference

Notes

Weekly Expense Tracker

 MON   SEPTEMBER 2, 2019   **TUE**   SEPTEMBER 3, 2019   **WED**   SEPTEMBER 4, 2019

Description	Amount	Description	Amount	Description	Amount
Total		Total		Total	

 THU   SEPTEMBER 5, 2019   **FRI**   SEPTEMBER 6, 2019   **SAT**   SEPTEMBER 7, 2019

Description	Amount	Description	Amount	Description	Amount
Total		Total		Total	

$ SUN $ SEPTEMBER 8, 2019

Description	Amount
Total	

Notes

Weekly Expense Tracker

MON SEPTEMBER 9, 2019   **TUE** SEPTEMBER 10, 2019   **WED** SEPTEMBER 11, 2019

Description	Amount	Description	Amount	Description	Amount
Total		Total		Total	

 THU SEPTEMBER 12, 2019   **FRI** SEPTEMBER 13, 2019   **SAT** SEPTEMBER 14, 2019

Description	Amount	Description	Amount	Description	Amount
Total		Total		Total	

 SUN SEPTEMBER 15, 2019

Description	Amount
Total	

Notes

Weekly Expense Tracker

MON SEPTEMBER 16, 2019

Description	Amount
Total	

TUE SEPTEMBER 17, 2019

Description	Amount
Total	

WED SEPTEMBER 18, 2019

Description	Amount
Total	

THU SEPTEMBER 19, 2019

Description	Amount
Total	

FRI SEPTEMBER 20, 2019

Description	Amount
Total	

SAT SEPTEMBER 21, 2019

Description	Amount
Total	

$ SUN $ SEPTEMBER 22, 2019

Description	Amount
Total	

Notes

Weekly Expense Tracker

MON SEPTEMBER 23, 2019   **TUE** SEPTEMBER 24, 2019   **WED** SEPTEMBER 25, 2019

Description	Amount	Description	Amount	Description	Amount
Total		Total		Total	

THU SEPTEMBER 26, 2019   **FRI** SEPTEMBER 27, 2019   **SAT** SEPTEMBER 28, 2019

Description	Amount	Description	Amount	Description	Amount
Total		Total		Total	

SUN SEPTEMBER 29, 2019

Description	Amount
Total	

Notes

_____

_____

_____

_____

_____

_____

_____

_____

_____

_____

_____

Weekly Expense Tracker

 MON   SEPTEMBER 30, 2019   **TUE**   OCTOBER 1, 2019   **WED**   OCTOBER 2, 2019

Description	Amount	Description	Amount	Description	Amount
Total		Total		Total	

 THU   OCTOBER 3, 2019   **FRI**   OCTOBER 4, 2019   **SAT**   OCTOBER 5, 2019

Description	Amount	Description	Amount	Description	Amount
Total		Total		Total	

$ **SUN** $ OCTOBER 6, 2019

Description	Amount
Total	

Notes

_____
_____
_____
_____
_____
_____
_____
_____
_____
_____
_____
_____

Note

October 2019

Sunday	Monday	Tuesday	Wednesday
29	30	1	2
	Rosh Hashanah		
6	7	8	9
			Yom Kippur
13	14	15	16
	Columbus Day		*Boss's Day*
20	21	22	23
27	28	29	30

Thursday	Friday	Saturday

September 2019

Su	M	Tu	W	Th	F	Sa
1	2	3	4	5	6	7
8	9	10	11	12	13	14
15	16	17	18	19	20	21
22	23	24	25	26	27	28
29	30					

3

4

5

10

11

12

17

18

19

24

25

26

United Nations Day

31

1

2

Halloween

November 2019

Su	M	Tu	W	Th	F	Sa
					1	2
3	4	5	6	7	8	9
10	11	12	13	14	15	16
17	18	19	20	21	22	23
24	25	26	27	28	29	30

Monthly Budget

Income		
Income 1		
Income 1		
Other Income		
Total Income		

Goal :

Budget :

Bill To Be Paid	Date Due	Amount	Paid	Note
			○	
			○	
			○	
			○	
			○	
			○	
			○	
			○	
			○	
			○	
			○	
			○	
			○	
			○	
			○	
			○	
			○	
			○	
			○	
			○	
			○	
			○	
			○	
			○	
Total				

Monthly Budget

Other Expenses	Date	Amount	Note
Total			

Total Income

Total Expenses

Difference

Notes

Weekly Expense Tracker

 MON OCTOBER 7, 2019   **TUE** OCTOBER 8, 2019   **WED** OCTOBER 9, 2019

Description	Amount	Description	Amount	Description	Amount
Total		**Total**		**Total**	

 THU OCTOBER 10, 2019   **FRI** OCTOBER 11, 2019   **SAT** OCTOBER 12, 2019

Description	Amount	Description	Amount	Description	Amount
Total		**Total**		**Total**	

$ **SUN** $ OCTOBER 13, 2019

Description	Amount
Total	

Notes

_____

_____

_____

_____

_____

_____

_____

_____

_____

Weekly Expense Tracker

MON OCTOBER 14, 2019

Description	Amount
Total	

TUE OCTOBER 15, 2019

Description	Amount
Total	

WED OCTOBER 16, 2019

Description	Amount
Total	

THU OCTOBER 17, 2019

Description	Amount
Total	

FRI OCTOBER 18, 2019

Description	Amount
Total	

SAT OCTOBER 19, 2019

Description	Amount
Total	

SUN OCTOBER 20, 2019

Description	Amount
Total	

Notes

Weekly Expense Tracker

 MON OCTOBER 21, 2019   **TUE** OCTOBER 22, 2019   **WED** OCTOBER 23, 2019

Description	Amount	Description	Amount	Description	Amount
Total		**Total**		**Total**	

 THU OCTOBER 24, 2019   **FRI** OCTOBER 25, 2019   **SAT** OCTOBER 26, 2019

Description	Amount	Description	Amount	Description	Amount
Total		**Total**		**Total**	

$ SUN $ OCTOBER 27, 2019

Description	Amount
Total	

Notes

Weekly Expense Tracker

MON OCTOBER 28, 2019

Description	Amount
Total	

 TUE OCTOBER 29, 2019

Description	Amount
Total	

WED OCTOBER 30, 2019

Description	Amount
Total	

THU OCTOBER 31, 2019

Description	Amount
Total	

FRI NOVEMBER 1, 2019

Description	Amount
Total	

SAT NOVEMBER 2, 2019

Description	Amount
Total	

SUN NOVEMBER 3, 2019

Description	Amount
Total	

Notes

November 2019

Sunday	Monday	Tuesday	Wednesday
27	28	29	30
3 *Daylight Saving*	4	5	6
10	11 *Veterans Day*	12	13
17	18	19	20
24	25	26	27

Thursday	Friday	Saturday
31	1	2
Halloween		
7	8	9
14	15	16
21	22	23
28	29	30
Thanksgiving		

October 2019

Su	M	Tu	W	Th	F	Sa
	1	2	3	4	5
6	7	8	9	10	11	12
13	14	15	16	17	18	19
20	21	22	23	24	25	26
27	28	29	30	31		

December 2019

Su	M	Tu	W	Th	F	Sa
1	2	3	4	5	6	7
8	9	10	11	12	13	14
15	16	17	18	19	20	21
22	23	24	25	26	27	28
29	30	31				

Monthly Budget

Income		
Income 1		
Income 1		
Other Income		
Total Income		

Goal :

Budget :

Bill To Be Paid	Date Due	Amount	Paid	Note
			○	
			○	
			○	
			○	
			○	
			○	
			○	
			○	
			○	
			○	
			○	
			○	
			○	
			○	
			○	
			○	
			○	
			○	
			○	
			○	
			○	
			○	
			○	
			○	
Total				

Monthly Budget

Other Expenses	Date	Amount	Note
Total			

Total Income

Total Expenses

Difference

Notes

Weekly Expense Tracker

 MON NOVEMBER 4, 2019   **TUE** NOVEMBER 5, 2019   **WED** NOVEMBER 6, 2019

Description	Amount		Description	Amount		Description	Amount
Total			**Total**			**Total**	

 THU NOVEMBER 7, 2019   **FRI** NOVEMBER 8, 2019   **SAT** NOVEMBER 9, 2019

Description	Amount		Description	Amount		Description	Amount
Total			**Total**			**Total**	

$ SUN $ NOVEMBER 10, 2019

Notes

Description	Amount
Total	

Weekly Expense Tracker

MON NOVEMBER 11, 2019 **TUE** NOVEMBER 12, 2019 **WED** NOVEMBER 13, 2019

Description	Amount	Description	Amount	Description	Amount
Total		Total		Total	

THU NOVEMBER 14, 2019 **FRI** NOVEMBER 15, 2019 **SAT** NOVEMBER 16, 2019

Description	Amount	Description	Amount	Description	Amount
Total		Total		Total	

SUN NOVEMBER 17, 2019

Description	Amount
Total	

Notes

_____
_____
_____
_____
_____
_____
_____
_____
_____
_____

Weekly Expense Tracker

 MON   NOVEMBER 18, 2019   **TUE**   NOVEMBER 19, 2019   **WED**   NOVEMBER 20, 2019

Description	Amount	Description	Amount	Description	Amount
Total		**Total**		**Total**	

 THU   NOVEMBER 21, 2019   **FRI**   NOVEMBER 22, 2019   **SAT**   NOVEMBER 23, 2019

Description	Amount	Description	Amount	Description	Amount
Total		**Total**		**Total**	

$ SUN $ NOVEMBER 24, 2019

Description	Amount
Total	

Notes

_____
_____
_____
_____
_____
_____
_____
_____
_____
_____
_____

Weekly Expense Tracker

MON NOVEMBER 25, 2019   **TUE** NOVEMBER 26, 2019   **WED** NOVEMBER 27, 2019

Description	Amount		Description	Amount		Description	Amount
Total			**Total**			**Total**	

THU NOVEMBER 28, 2019   **FRI** NOVEMBER 29, 2019   **SAT** NOVEMBER 30, 2019

Description	Amount		Description	Amount		Description	Amount
Total			**Total**			**Total**	

SUN DECEMBER 1, 2019

Description	Amount
Total	

Notes

_____

_____

_____

_____

_____

_____

_____

_____

_____

December 2019

Sunday	Monday	Tuesday	Wednesday
1	2	3	4
8	9	10	11
15	16	17	18
22 Dec. Solstice Hanukkah begins	23	24 Christmas Eve	25 Christmas Day
29	30	31 New Year's Eve	1 New Year's Day

Thursday	Friday	Saturday
5	6	7 *Pearl Harbor*
12	13	14
19	20	21
26 *Boxing Day (UK)* *Kwanzaa begins*	27	28
2	3	4

November 2019

Su	M	Tu	W	Th	F	Sa
					1	2
3	4	5	6	7	8	9
10	11	12	13	14	15	16
17	18	19	20	21	22	23
24	25	26	27	28	29	30

January 2020

Su	M	Tu	W	Th	F	Sa
			1	2	3	4
5	6	7	8	9	10	11
12	13	14	15	16	17	18
19	20	21	22	23	24	25
26	27	28	29	30	31	

Monthly Budget

Income		
Income 1		
Income 1		
Other Income		
Total Income		

Goal :

Budget :

Bill To Be Paid	Date Due	Amount	Paid	Note
			◯	
			◯	
			◯	
			◯	
			◯	
			◯	
			◯	
			◯	
			◯	
			◯	
			◯	
			◯	
			◯	
			◯	
			◯	
			◯	
			◯	
			◯	
			◯	
			◯	
			◯	
			◯	
			◯	
Total				

Monthly Budget

Other Expenses	Date	Amount	Note
Total			

Total Income

Total Expenses

Difference

Notes

Weekly Expense Tracker

 MON DECEMBER 2, 2019   **TUE** DECEMBER 3, 2019   **WED** DECEMBER 4, 2019

Description	Amount	Description	Amount	Description	Amount
Total		**Total**		**Total**	

 THU DECEMBER 5, 2019   **FRI** DECEMBER 6, 2019   **SAT** DECEMBER 7, 2019

Description	Amount	Description	Amount	Description	Amount
Total		**Total**		**Total**	

$ SUN $ DECEMBER 8, 2019

Description	Amount
Total	

Notes

_____

_____

_____

_____

_____

_____

_____

_____

_____

Weekly Expense Tracker

MON DECEMBER 9, 2019   **TUE** DECEMBER 10, 2019   **WED** DECEMBER 11, 2019

Description	Amount	Description	Amount	Description	Amount
Total		**Total**		**Total**	

THU DECEMBER 12, 2019   **FRI** DECEMBER 13, 2019   **SAT** DECEMBER 14, 2019

Description	Amount	Description	Amount	Description	Amount
Total		**Total**		**Total**	

SUN DECEMBER 15, 2019

Description	Amount
Total	

Notes

Weekly Expense Tracker

 MON   DECEMBER 16, 2019

Description	Amount
Total	

 TUE   DECEMBER 17, 2019

Description	Amount
Total	

 WED   DECEMBER 18, 2019

Description	Amount
Total	

 THU   DECEMBER 19, 2019

Description	Amount
Total	

 FRI   DECEMBER 20, 2019

Description	Amount
Total	

 SAT   DECEMBER 21, 2019

Description	Amount
Total	

$ SUN $ DECEMBER 22, 2019

Description	Amount
Total	

Notes

Weekly Expense Tracker

MON   DECEMBER 23, 2019   **TUE**   DECEMBER 24, 2019   **WED**   DECEMBER 25, 2019

Description	Amount	Description	Amount	Description	Amount
Total		Total		Total	

THU   DECEMBER 26, 2019   **FRI**   DECEMBER 27, 2019   **SAT**   DECEMBER 28, 2019

Description	Amount	Description	Amount	Description	Amount
Total		Total		Total	

SUN   DECEMBER 29, 2019

Description	Amount
Total	

Notes

_____
_____
_____
_____
_____
_____
_____
_____
_____
_____
_____
_____

Weekly Expense Tracker

 MON   DECEMBER 30, 2019   **TUE**   DECEMBER 31, 2019   **WED**   JANUARY 1, 2020

Description	Amount		Description	Amount		Description	Amount
Total			**Total**			**Total**	

 THU   JANUARY 2, 2020   **FRI**   JANUARY 3, 2020   **SAT**   JANUARY 4, 2020

Description	Amount		Description	Amount		Description	Amount
Total			**Total**			**Total**	

$ SUN $ JANUARY 5, 2020

Description	Amount
Total	

Notes

Note

January 2020

Sunday	Monday	Tuesday	Wednesday
29	30	31	1 *New Year's Day*
5	6	7	8
12	13	14	15
19	20 *M.L. King Day*	21	22
26	27	28	29

December 2019

Su	M	Tu	W	Th	F	Sa
1	2	3	4	5	6	7
8	9	10	11	12	13	14
15	16	17	18	19	20	21
22	23	24	25	26	27	28
29	30	31				

Thursday	Friday	Saturday
2	3	4
9	10	11
16	17	18
23	24	25 Chinese New Year
30	31	1

February 2020

Su	M	Tu	W	Th	F	Sa
						1
2	3	4	5	6	7	8
9	10	11	12	13	14	15
16	17	18	19	20	21	22
23	24	25	26	27	28	29

Monthly Budget

Income		
Income 1		
Income 1		
Other Income		
Total Income		

Goal :

Budget :

Bill To Be Paid	Date Due	Amount	Paid	Note
			○	
			○	
			○	
			○	
			○	
			○	
			○	
			○	
			○	
			○	
			○	
			○	
			○	
			○	
			○	
			○	
			○	
			○	
			○	
			○	
			○	
			○	
			○	
Total				

Monthly Budget

Other Expenses	Date	Amount	Note
Total			

Total Income

Total Expenses

Difference

Notes

Weekly Expense Tracker

 MON   JANUARY 6, 2020   **TUE**   JANUARY 7, 2020   **WED**   JANUARY 8, 2020

Description	Amount		Description	Amount		Description	Amount
Total			**Total**			**Total**	

 THU   JANUARY 9, 2020   **FRI**   JANUARY 10, 2020   **SAT**   JANUARY 11, 2020

Description	Amount		Description	Amount		Description	Amount
Total			**Total**			**Total**	

$ SUN $ JANUARY 12, 2020

Description	Amount
Total	

Notes

Weekly Expense Tracker

MON JANUARY 13, 2020

Description	Amount
Total	

TUE JANUARY 14, 2020

Description	Amount
Total	

WED JANUARY 15, 2020

Description	Amount
Total	

THU JANUARY 16, 2020

Description	Amount
Total	

FRI JANUARY 17, 2020

Description	Amount
Total	

SAT JANUARY 18, 2020

Description	Amount
Total	

SUN JANUARY 19, 2020

Description	Amount
Total	

Notes

Weekly Expense Tracker

 MON   JANUARY 20, 2020   **TUE**   JANUARY 21, 2020   **WED**   JANUARY 22, 2020

Description	Amount	Description	Amount	Description	Amount
Total		Total		Total	

 THU   JANUARY 23, 2020   **FRI**   JANUARY 24, 2020   **SAT**   JANUARY 25, 2020

Description	Amount	Description	Amount	Description	Amount
Total		Total		Total	

$ SUN $ JANUARY 26, 2020

Description	Amount
Total	

Notes

_____

_____

_____

_____

_____

_____

_____

_____

_____

_____

_____

Weekly Expense Tracker

MON JANUARY 27, 2020   **TUE** JANUARY 28, 2020   **WED** JANUARY 29, 2020

Description	Amount	Description	Amount	Description	Amount
Total		**Total**		**Total**	

 THU JANUARY 30, 2020   **FRI** JANUARY 31, 2020   **SAT** FEBRUARY 1, 2020

Description	Amount	Description	Amount	Description	Amount
Total		**Total**		**Total**	

SUN FEBRUARY 2, 2020

Description	Amount
Total	

Notes

_____
_____
_____
_____
_____
_____
_____
_____
_____
_____

february 2020

Sunday	Monday	Tuesday	Wednesday
26	27	28	29
2 *Groundhog Day*	3	4	5
9	10	11	12 *Lincoln's B-Day*
16	17 *Presidents' Day*	18	19
23	24	25 *Mardi Gras*	26 *Ash Wednesday*

Thursday	Friday	Saturday
30	31	1
6	7	8
13	14 *Valentine's Day*	15
20	21	22
27	28	29

Monthly Budget

Income		
Income 1		
Income 1		
Other Income		
Total Income		

Goal :

Budget :

Bill To Be Paid	Date Due	Amount	Paid	Note
			◯	
			◯	
			◯	
			◯	
			◯	
			◯	
			◯	
			◯	
			◯	
			◯	
			◯	
			◯	
			◯	
			◯	
			◯	
			◯	
			◯	
			◯	
			◯	
			◯	
			◯	
			◯	
			◯	
Total				

Monthly Budget

Other Expenses	Date	Amount	Note
Total			

Total Income

Total Expenses

Difference

Notes

Weekly Expense Tracker

 MON   FEBRUARY 3, 2020   **TUE**   FEBRUARY 4, 2020   **WED**   FEBRUARY 5, 2020

Description	Amount	Description	Amount	Description	Amount
Total		**Total**		**Total**	

 THU   FEBRUARY 6, 2020   **FRI**   FEBRUARY 7, 2020   **SAT**   FEBRUARY 8, 2020

Description	Amount	Description	Amount	Description	Amount
Total		**Total**		**Total**	

$ SUN $ FEBRUARY 9, 2020

Description	Amount
Total	

Notes

Weekly Expense Tracker

 MON   FEBRUARY 10, 2020   **TUE**   FEBRUARY 11, 2020   **WED**   FEBRUARY 12, 2020

Description	Amount	Description	Amount	Description	Amount
Total		**Total**		**Total**	

 THU   FEBRUARY 13, 2020   **FRI**   FEBRUARY 14, 2020   **SAT**   FEBRUARY 15, 2020

Description	Amount	Description	Amount	Description	Amount
Total		**Total**		**Total**	

SUN   FEBRUARY 16, 2020

Description	Amount
Total	

Notes

_____
_____
_____
_____
_____
_____
_____
_____
_____

Weekly Expense Tracker

 MON FEBRUARY 17, 2020   **TUE** FEBRUARY 18, 2020   **WED** FEBRUARY 19, 2020

Description	Amount	Description	Amount	Description	Amount
Total		Total		Total	

 THU FEBRUARY 20, 2020   **FRI** FEBRUARY 21, 2020   **SAT** FEBRUARY 22, 2020

Description	Amount	Description	Amount	Description	Amount
Total		Total		Total	

$ SUN $ FEBRUARY 23, 2020

Description	Amount
Total	

Notes

Weekly Expense Tracker

 MON FEBRUARY 24, 2020   **TUE** FEBRUARY 25, 2020   **WED** FEBRUARY 26, 2020

Description	Amount		Description	Amount		Description	Amount
Total			Total			Total	

 THU FEBRUARY 27, 2020   **FRI** FEBRUARY 28, 2020   **SAT** FEBRUARY 29, 2020

Description	Amount		Description	Amount		Description	Amount
Total			Total			Total	

SUN MARCH 1, 2020

Description	Amount
Total	

Notes

_____
_____
_____
_____
_____
_____
_____
_____
_____
_____
_____

March 2020

Sunday	Monday	Tuesday	Wednesday
1	2	3	4
8 *Daylight Saving*	9	10	11
15	16	17 *St. Patrick's Day*	18
22	23	24	25
29	30	31	1 *April Fool's Day*

Thursday	Friday	Saturday
5	6	7
12	13	14
19	20 *Vernal equinox*	21
26	27	28
2	3	4

February 2020

Su	M	Tu	W	Th	F	Sa
						1
2	3	4	5	6	7	8
9	10	11	12	13	14	15
16	17	18	19	20	21	22
23	24	25	26	27	28	29

April 2020

Su	M	Tu	W	Th	F	Sa
			1	2	3	4
5	6	7	8	9	10	11
12	13	14	15	16	17	18
19	20	21	22	23	24	25
26	27	28	29	30		

Monthly Budget

Income		
Income 1		
Income 1		
Other Income		
Total Income		

Goal :

Budget :

Bill To Be Paid	Date Due	Amount	Paid	Note
			○	
			○	
			○	
			○	
			○	
			○	
			○	
			○	
			○	
			○	
			○	
			○	
			○	
			○	
			○	
			○	
			○	
			○	
			○	
			○	
			○	
			○	
			○	
Total				

Monthly Budget

Other Expenses	Date	Amount	Note
Total			

Total Income

Total Expenses

Difference

Notes

_____

_____

_____

_____

_____

_____

Weekly Expense Tracker

 MON   **MARCH 2, 2020**

Description	Amount
Total	

 TUE   **MARCH 3, 2020**

Description	Amount
Total	

 WED   **MARCH 4, 2020**

Description	Amount
Total	

 THU   **MARCH 5, 2020**

Description	Amount
Total	

 FRI   **MARCH 6, 2020**

Description	Amount
Total	

 SAT   **MARCH 7, 2020**

Description	Amount
Total	

$ SUN $ **MARCH 8, 2020**

Description	Amount
Total	

Notes

Weekly Expense Tracker

 MON MARCH 9, 2020   **TUE** MARCH 10, 2020   **WED** MARCH 11, 2020

Description	Amount	Description	Amount	Description	Amount
Total		Total		Total	

THU MARCH 12, 2020   **FRI** MARCH 13, 2020   **SAT** MARCH 14, 2020

Description	Amount	Description	Amount	Description	Amount
Total		Total		Total	

SUN MARCH 15, 2020

Description	Amount
Total	

Notes

Weekly Expense Tracker

 MON   MARCH 16, 2020   **TUE**   MARCH 17, 2020   **WED**   MARCH 18, 2020

Description	Amount		Description	Amount		Description	Amount
Total			**Total**			**Total**	

 THU   MARCH 19, 2020   **FRI**   MARCH 20, 2020   **SAT**   MARCH 21, 2020

Description	Amount		Description	Amount		Description	Amount
Total			**Total**			**Total**	

$ SUN $ MARCH 22, 2020

Description	Amount
Total	

Notes

_____
_____
_____
_____
_____
_____
_____
_____
_____
_____
_____

Weekly Expense Tracker

 MON MARCH 23, 2020   **TUE** MARCH 24, 2020   **WED** MARCH 25, 2020

Description	Amount		Description	Amount		Description	Amount
Total			**Total**			**Total**	

THU MARCH 26, 2020   **FRI** MARCH 27, 2020   **SAT** MARCH 28, 2020

Description	Amount		Description	Amount		Description	Amount
Total			**Total**			**Total**	

SUN MARCH 29, 2020

Description	Amount
Total	

Notes

_____
_____
_____
_____
_____
_____
_____
_____
_____
_____
_____

Weekly Expense Tracker

 MON   MARCH 30, 2020   **TUE**   MARCH 31, 2020   **WED**   APRIL 1, 2020

Description	Amount	Description	Amount	Description	Amount
Total		**Total**		**Total**	

 THU   APRIL 2, 2020   **FRI**   APRIL 3, 2020   **SAT**   APRIL 4, 2020

Description	Amount	Description	Amount	Description	Amount
Total		**Total**		**Total**	

$ SUN $ APRIL 5, 2020

Description	Amount
Total	

Notes

_____

_____

_____

_____

_____

_____

_____

_____

_____

Note

April 2020

Sunday	Monday	Tuesday	Wednesday
29	30	31	1 *April Fool's Day*
5	6	7	8
12 *Easter*	13 *Easter Monday (U.K.)*	14	15 *Taxes Due*
19	20	21	22 *Earth Day* *Admin Assist Day*
26	27	28	29

Thursday	Friday	Saturday
2	3	4

March 2020

Su	M	Tu	W	Th	F	Sa
1	2	3	4	5	6	7
8	9	10	11	12	13	14
15	16	17	18	19	20	21
22	23	24	25	26	27	28
29	30	31				

9	10	11
Passover	*Good Friday*	
16	17	18
23	24	25
	Ramadan begins	
30	1	2

May 2020

Su	M	Tu	W	Th	F	Sa
					1	2
3	4	5	6	7	8	9
10	11	12	13	14	15	16
17	18	19	20	21	22	23
24	25	26	27	28	29	30
31						

Monthly Budget

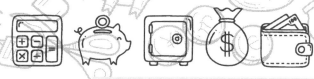

Income		
Income 1		
Income 1		
Other Income		
Total Income		

Goal : _____

Budget : _____

Bill To Be Paid	Date Due	Amount	Paid	Note
			◯	
			◯	
			◯	
			◯	
			◯	
			◯	
			◯	
			◯	
			◯	
			◯	
			◯	
			◯	
			◯	
			◯	
			◯	
			◯	
			◯	
			◯	
			◯	
			◯	
			◯	
			◯	
			◯	
			◯	
Total				

Monthly Budget

Other Expenses	Date	Amount	Note
Total			

Total Income

Total Expenses

Difference

Notes

Weekly Expense Tracker

MON   APRIL 6, 2020

Description	Amount
Total	

TUE   APRIL 7, 2020

Description	Amount
Total	

WED   APRIL 8, 2020

Description	Amount
Total	

THU   APRIL 9, 2020

Description	Amount
Total	

FRI   APRIL 10, 2020

Description	Amount
Total	

SAT   APRIL 11, 2020

Description	Amount
Total	

$ SUN $ APRIL 12, 2020

Description	Amount
Total	

Notes

_____
_____
_____
_____
_____
_____
_____
_____
_____
_____
_____
_____

Weekly Expense Tracker

MON APRIL 13, 2020 **TUE** APRIL 14, 2020 **WED** APRIL 15, 2020

Description	Amount
Total	

Description	Amount
Total	

Description	Amount
Total	

THU APRIL 16, 2020 **FRI** APRIL 17, 2020 **SAT** APRIL 18, 2020

Description	Amount
Total	

Description	Amount
Total	

Description	Amount
Total	

SUN APRIL 19, 2020

Description	Amount
Total	

Notes

Weekly Expense Tracker

MON APRIL 20, 2020

Description	Amount
Total	

TUE APRIL 21, 2020

Description	Amount
Total	

WED APRIL 22, 2020

Description	Amount
Total	

THU APRIL 23, 2020

Description	Amount
Total	

FRI APRIL 24, 2020

Description	Amount
Total	

SAT APRIL 25, 2020

Description	Amount
Total	

$ SUN $ APRIL 26, 2020

Description	Amount
Total	

Notes

Weekly Expense Tracker

 MON   APRIL 27, 2020

Description	Amount
Total	

 TUE   APRIL 28, 2020

Description	Amount
Total	

WED   APRIL 29, 2020

Description	Amount
Total	

THU   APRIL 30, 2020

Description	Amount
Total	

FRI   MAY 1, 2020

Description	Amount
Total	

SAT   MAY 2, 2020

Description	Amount
Total	

SUN   MAY 3, 2020

Description	Amount
Total	

Notes

May 2020

Sunday	Monday	Tuesday	Wednesday
26	27	28	29
3	4 *May Day (U.K.)*	5 *Cinco de Mayo*	6
10 *Mother's Day*	11	12	13
17	18 *Victoria Day (Canada)*	19	20
24 *End of Ramadan*	25 *Memorial Day*	26	27
31 *Pentecost*	1	2	3

Thursday	Friday	Saturday
30	1	2
7	8	9
14	15	16
21	22	23 *Armed Forces Day*
28	29	30
4	5	6

April 2020

Su	M	Tu	W	Th	F	Sa
			1	2	3	4
5	6	7	8	9	10	11
12	13	14	15	16	17	18
19	20	21	22	23	24	25
26	27	28	29	30		

June 2020

Su	M	Tu	W	Th	F	Sa
	1	2	3	4	5	6
7	8	9	10	11	12	13
14	15	16	17	18	19	20
21	22	23	24	25	26	27
28	29	30				

Monthly Budget

Income		
Income 1		
Income 1		
Other Income		
Total Income		

Goal : _____

Budget : _____

Bill To Be Paid	Date Due	Amount	Paid	Note
			◯	
			◯	
			◯	
			◯	
			◯	
			◯	
			◯	
			◯	
			◯	
			◯	
			◯	
			◯	
			◯	
			◯	
			◯	
			◯	
			◯	
			◯	
			◯	
			◯	
			◯	
			◯	
			◯	
Total				

Monthly Budget

Other Expenses	Date	Amount	Note
Total			

Total Income

Total Expenses

Difference

Notes

Weekly Expense Tracker

 MON MAY 4, 2020

Description	Amount
Total	

 TUE MAY 5, 2020

Description	Amount
Total	

WED MAY 6, 2020

Description	Amount
Total	

 THU MAY 7, 2020

Description	Amount
Total	

 FRI MAY 8, 2020

Description	Amount
Total	

 SAT MAY 9, 2020

Description	Amount
Total	

$ SUN $ MAY 10, 2020

Description	Amount
Total	

Notes

_____
_____
_____
_____
_____
_____
_____
_____
_____
_____
_____
_____

Weekly Expense Tracker

 MON   MAY 11, 2020

Description	Amount
Total	

 TUE   MAY 12, 2020

Description	Amount
Total	

WED   MAY 13, 2020

Description	Amount
Total	

THU   MAY 14, 2020

Description	Amount
Total	

FRI   MAY 15, 2020

Description	Amount
Total	

SAT   MAY 16, 2020

Description	Amount
Total	

SUN   MAY 17, 2020

Description	Amount
Total	

Notes

Weekly Expense Tracker

 MON MAY 18, 2020

Description	Amount
Total	

 TUE MAY 19, 2020

Description	Amount
Total	

WED MAY 20, 2020

Description	Amount
Total	

 THU MAY 21, 2020

Description	Amount
Total	

 FRI MAY 22, 2020

Description	Amount
Total	

 SAT MAY 23, 2020

Description	Amount
Total	

SUN MAY 24, 2020

Description	Amount
Total	

Notes

_____
_____
_____
_____
_____
_____
_____
_____
_____
_____
_____
_____
_____

Weekly Expense Tracker

MON   MAY 25, 2020

Description	Amount
Total	

TUE   MAY 26, 2020

Description	Amount
Total	

WED   MAY 27, 2020

Description	Amount
Total	

THU   MAY 28, 2020

Description	Amount
Total	

FRI   MAY 29, 2020

Description	Amount
Total	

SAT   MAY 30, 2020

Description	Amount
Total	

SUN   MAY 31, 2020

Description	Amount
Total	

Notes

_____
_____
_____
_____
_____
_____
_____
_____
_____
_____
_____
_____
_____
_____

June 2020

Sunday	Monday	Tuesday	Wednesday
31	1	2	3
7 *Pentecost*	8	9	10
14	15	16	17
21 *Flag Day*	22	23	24
28 *Father's Day*	29	30	1

Thursday	Friday	Saturday
4	5	6
11	12	13
18	19	20
25	26	27
2	3	4

June Solstice

Independence Day

May 2020

Su	M	Tu	W	Th	F	Sa
					1	2
3	4	5	6	7	8	9
10	11	12	13	14	15	16
17	18	19	20	21	22	23
24	25	26	27	28	29	30
31						

July 2020

Su	M	Tu	W	Th	F	Sa
			1	2	3	4
5	6	7	8	9	10	11
12	13	14	15	16	17	18
19	20	21	22	23	24	25
26	27	28	29	30	31	

Monthly Budget

Income		
Income 1		
Income 1		
Other Income		
Total Income		

Goal :

Budget :

Bill To Be Paid	Date Due	Amount	Paid	Note
			◯	
			◯	
			◯	
			◯	
			◯	
			◯	
			◯	
			◯	
			◯	
			◯	
			◯	
			◯	
			◯	
			◯	
			◯	
			◯	
			◯	
			◯	
			◯	
			◯	
			◯	
			◯	
			◯	
Total				

Monthly Budget

Other Expenses	Date	Amount	Note
Total			

Total Income

Total Expenses

Difference

Notes

Weekly Expense Tracker

MON   JUNE 1, 2020

Description	Amount
Total	

TUE   JUNE 2, 2020

Description	Amount
Total	

WED   JUNE 3, 2020

Description	Amount
Total	

THU   JUNE 4, 2020

Description	Amount
Total	

FRI   JUNE 5, 2020

Description	Amount
Total	

SAT   JUNE 6, 2020

Description	Amount
Total	

SUN   JUNE 7, 2020

Description	Amount
Total	

Notes

_____
_____
_____
_____
_____
_____
_____
_____
_____
_____

Weekly Expense Tracker

 MON   JUNE 8, 2020   **TUE**   JUNE 9, 2020   **WED**   JUNE 10, 2020

Description	Amount		Description	Amount		Description	Amount
Total			Total			Total	

THU   JUNE 11, 2020   **FRI**   JUNE 12, 2020   **SAT**   JUNE 13, 2020

Description	Amount		Description	Amount		Description	Amount
Total			Total			Total	

SUN   JUNE 14, 2020

Description	Amount
Total	

Notes

Weekly Expense Tracker

MON   JUNE 15, 2020

Description	Amount
Total	

TUE   JUNE 16, 2020

Description	Amount
Total	

WED   JUNE 17, 2020

Description	Amount
Total	

THU   JUNE 18, 2020

Description	Amount
Total	

FRI   JUNE 19, 2020

Description	Amount
Total	

SAT   JUNE 20, 2020

Description	Amount
Total	

$ SUN $ JUNE 21, 2020

Description	Amount
Total	

Notes

_____
_____
_____
_____
_____
_____
_____
_____
_____
_____
_____
_____

Weekly Expense Tracker

 MON   JUNE 22, 2020   **TUE**   JUNE 23, 2020   **WED**   JUNE 24, 2020

Description	Amount	Description	Amount	Description	Amount
Total		**Total**		**Total**	

THU   JUNE 25, 2020   **FRI**   JUNE 26, 2020   **SAT**   JUNE 27, 2020

Description	Amount	Description	Amount	Description	Amount
Total		**Total**		**Total**	

SUN   JUNE 28, 2020

Description	Amount
Total	

Notes

_____
_____
_____
_____
_____
_____
_____
_____
_____
_____

Weekly Expense Tracker

MON — JUNE 29, 2020

Description	Amount
Total	

TUE — JUNE 30, 2020

Description	Amount
Total	

WED — JULY 1, 2020

Description	Amount
Total	

 THU — JULY 2, 2020

Description	Amount
Total	

 FRI — JULY 3, 2020

Description	Amount
Total	

 SAT — JULY 4, 2020

Description	Amount
Total	

$ SUN $ — JULY 5, 2020

Description	Amount
Total	

Notes

Note

July 2020

Sunday	Monday	Tuesday	Wednesday
28	29	30	1
5	6	7	8
12	13	14	15
19	20	21	22
26	27	28	29

Parents' Day

Thursday	Friday	Saturday
2	3	4
		Independence Day
9	10	11
16	17	18
23	24	25
30	31	1

June 2020

Su	M	Tu	W	Th	F	Sa
	1	2	3	4	5	6
7	8	9	10	11	12	13
14	15	16	17	18	19	20
21	22	23	24	25	26	27
28	29	30				

August 2020

Su	M	Tu	W	Th	F	Sa
						1
2	3	4	5	6	7	8
9	10	11	12	13	14	15
16	17	18	19	20	21	22
23	24	25	26	27	28	29
30	31					

Monthly Budget

Income		
Income 1		
Income 1		
Other Income		
Total Income		

Goal :

Budget :

Bill To Be Paid	Date Due	Amount	Paid	Note
			○	
			○	
			○	
			○	
			○	
			○	
			○	
			○	
			○	
			○	
			○	
			○	
			○	
			○	
			○	
			○	
			○	
			○	
			○	
			○	
			○	
			○	
			○	
			○	
Total				

Monthly Budget

Other Expenses	Date	Amount	Note
Total			

Total Income

Total Expenses

Difference

Notes

Weekly Expense Tracker

MON   JULY 6, 2020

Description	Amount
Total	

TUE   JULY 7, 2020

Description	Amount
Total	

WED   JULY 8, 2020

Description	Amount
Total	

THU   JULY 9, 2020

Description	Amount
Total	

FRI   JULY 10, 2020

Description	Amount
Total	

SAT   JULY 11, 2020

Description	Amount
Total	

$ SUN $ JULY 12, 2020

Description	Amount
Total	

Notes

Weekly Expense Tracker

 MON   JULY 13, 2020   **TUE**   JULY 14, 2020   **WED**   JULY 15, 2020

Description	Amount		Description	Amount		Description	Amount
Total			Total			Total	

THU   JULY 16, 2020   **FRI**   JULY 17, 2020   **SAT**   JULY 18, 2020

Description	Amount		Description	Amount		Description	Amount
Total			Total			Total	

SUN   JULY 19, 2020

Description	Amount
Total	

Notes

_____
_____
_____
_____
_____
_____
_____
_____
_____
_____
_____

Weekly Expense Tracker

 MON · JULY 20, 2020

Description	Amount
Total	

 TUE · JULY 21, 2020

Description	Amount
Total	

 WED · JULY 22, 2020

Description	Amount
Total	

 THU · JULY 23, 2020

Description	Amount
Total	

 FRI · JULY 24, 2020

Description	Amount
Total	

 SAT · JULY 25, 2020

Description	Amount
Total	

SUN · JULY 26, 2020

Description	Amount
Total	

Notes

Weekly Expense Tracker

 MON   JULY 27, 2020   **TUE**   JULY 28, 2020   **WED**   JULY 29, 2020

Description	Amount		Description	Amount		Description	Amount
Total			**Total**			**Total**	

THU   JULY 30, 2020   **FRI**   JULY 31, 2020   **SAT**   AUGUST 1, 2020

Description	Amount		Description	Amount		Description	Amount
Total			**Total**			**Total**	

SUN   AUGUST 2, 2020

Description	Amount
Total	

Notes

_____
_____
_____
_____
_____
_____
_____
_____
_____
_____
_____

August 2020

Sunday	Monday	Tuesday	Wednesday
26 *Parents' Day*	27	28	29
2	3 *Summer Bank Holiday (UK)*	4	5
9	10	11	12
16	17	18	19 *Aviation Day*
23	24	25	26
30	31 *Late Summer Bank Holiday (UK)*	1	2

Thursday	**Friday**	**Saturday**
30	31	1
6	7	8
13	14	15
20	21	22
27	28	29
3	4	5

July 2020

Su	M	Tu	W	Th	F	Sa
			1	2	3	4
5	6	7	8	9	10	11
12	13	14	15	16	17	18
19	20	21	22	23	24	25
26	27	28	29	30	31	

September 2020

Su	M	Tu	W	Th	F	Sa
		1	2	3	4	5
6	7	8	9	10	11	12
13	14	15	16	17	18	19
20	21	22	23	24	25	26
27	28	29	30			

Monthly Budget

Income		
Income 1		
Income 1		
Other Income		
Total Income		

Goal :

Budget :

Bill To Be Paid	Date Due	Amount	Paid	Note
			◯	
			◯	
			◯	
			◯	
			◯	
			◯	
			◯	
			◯	
			◯	
			◯	
			◯	
			◯	
			◯	
			◯	
			◯	
			◯	
			◯	
			◯	
			◯	
			◯	
			◯	
			◯	
			◯	
Total				

Monthly Budget

Other Expenses	Date	Amount	Note
Total			

Total Income

Total Expenses

Difference

Notes
_____
_____
_____
_____
_____

Weekly Expense Tracker

 MON   AUGUST 3, 2020   **TUE**   AUGUST 4, 2020   **WED**   AUGUST 5, 2020

Description	Amount	Description	Amount	Description	Amount
Total		**Total**		**Total**	

 THU   AUGUST 6, 2020   **FRI**   AUGUST 7, 2020   **SAT**   AUGUST 8, 2020

Description	Amount	Description	Amount	Description	Amount
Total		**Total**		**Total**	

$ SUN $ AUGUST 9, 2020

Description	Amount
Total	

Notes

_____
_____
_____
_____
_____
_____
_____
_____
_____
_____
_____

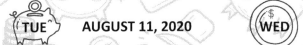
Weekly Expense Tracker

MON   AUGUST 10, 2020   **TUE**   AUGUST 11, 2020   **WED**   AUGUST 12, 2020

Description	Amount
Total	

Description	Amount
Total	

Description	Amount
Total	

THU   AUGUST 13, 2020   **FRI**   AUGUST 14, 2020   **SAT**   AUGUST 15, 2020

Description	Amount
Total	

Description	Amount
Total	

Description	Amount
Total	

SUN   AUGUST 16, 2020

Description	Amount
Total	

Notes

Weekly Expense Tracker

MON — AUGUST 17, 2020

Description	Amount
Total	

TUE — AUGUST 18, 2020

Description	Amount
Total	

WED — AUGUST 19, 2020

Description	Amount
Total	

THU — AUGUST 20, 2020

Description	Amount
Total	

FRI — AUGUST 21, 2020

Description	Amount
Total	

SAT — AUGUST 22, 2020

Description	Amount
Total	

$ SUN $ — AUGUST 23, 2020

Description	Amount
Total	

Notes

Weekly Expense Tracker

 MON AUGUST 24, 2020

Description	Amount
Total	

 TUE AUGUST 25, 2020

Description	Amount
Total	

WED AUGUST 26, 2020

Description	Amount
Total	

THU AUGUST 27, 2020

Description	Amount
Total	

FRI AUGUST 28, 2020

Description	Amount
Total	

SAT AUGUST 29, 2020

Description	Amount
Total	

SUN AUGUST 30, 2020

Description	Amount
Total	

Notes

Weekly Expense Tracker

 MON   AUGUST 31, 2020   **TUE**   SEPTEMBER 1, 2020   **WED**   SEPTEMBER 2, 2020

Description	Amount
Total	

Description	Amount
Total	

Description	Amount
Total	

 THU   SEPTEMBER 3, 2020   **FRI**   SEPTEMBER 4, 2020   **SAT**   SEPTEMBER 5, 2020

Description	Amount
Total	

Description	Amount
Total	

Description	Amount
Total	

$ SUN $ SEPTEMBER 6, 2020

Description	Amount
Total	

Notes

_____

_____

_____

_____

_____

_____

_____

_____

_____

_____

_____

_____

_____

Note

September 2020

Sunday	Monday	Tuesday	Wednesday
30	31	1	2
	Late Summer Bank Holiday (U.K.)		
6	7	8	9
	Labor Day		
13	14	15	16
Grandparents Day			
20	21	22	23
		Autumnal equinox	
27	28	29	30
	Yom Kippur		

Thursday	Friday	Saturday
3	4	5
10	11	12 *Patriot Day*
17	18	19 *Rosh Hashanah*
24 *Constitution Day*	25	26
1	2	3

August 2020

Su	M	Tu	W	Th	F	Sa
						1
2	3	4	5	6	7	8
9	10	11	12	13	14	15
16	17	18	19	20	21	22
23	24	25	26	27	28	29
30	31					

October 2020

Su	M	Tu	W	Th	F	Sa
				1	2	3
4	5	6	7	8	9	10
11	12	13	14	15	16	17
18	19	20	21	22	23	24
25	26	27	28	29	30	31

Monthly Budget

Income		
Income 1		
Income 1		
Other Income		
Total Income		

Goal :

Budget :

Bill To Be Paid	Date Due	Amount	Paid	Note
			○	
			○	
			○	
			○	
			○	
			○	
			○	
			○	
			○	
			○	
			○	
			○	
			○	
			○	
			○	
			○	
			○	
			○	
			○	
			○	
			○	
			○	
			○	
Total				

Monthly Budget

Other Expenses	Date	Amount	Note
Total			

Total Income

Total Expenses

Difference

Notes

_____

_____

_____

_____

_____

Weekly Expense Tracker

MON SEPTEMBER 7, 2020

Description	Amount
Total	

TUE SEPTEMBER 8, 2020

Description	Amount
Total	

WED SEPTEMBER 9, 2020

Description	Amount
Total	

THU SEPTEMBER 10, 2020

Description	Amount
Total	

FRI SEPTEMBER 11, 2020

Description	Amount
Total	

SAT SEPTEMBER 12, 2020

Description	Amount
Total	

$ SUN $ SEPTEMBER 13, 2020

Description	Amount
Total	

Notes

_____
_____
_____
_____
_____
_____
_____
_____
_____
_____
_____

Weekly Expense Tracker

MON SEPTEMBER 14, 2020 **TUE** SEPTEMBER 15, 2020 **WED** SEPTEMBER 16, 2020

Description	Amount
Total	

Description	Amount
Total	

Description	Amount
Total	

THU SEPTEMBER 17, 2020 **FRI** SEPTEMBER 18, 2020 **SAT** SEPTEMBER 19, 2020

Description	Amount
Total	

Description	Amount
Total	

Description	Amount
Total	

SUN SEPTEMBER 20, 2020

Description	Amount
Total	

Notes

Weekly Expense Tracker

MON SEPTEMBER 21, 2020   **TUE** SEPTEMBER 22, 2020   **WED** SEPTEMBER 23, 2020

Description	Amount	Description	Amount	Description	Amount
Total		**Total**		**Total**	

 THU SEPTEMBER 24, 2020   **FRI** SEPTEMBER 25, 2020   **SAT** SEPTEMBER 26, 2020

Description	Amount	Description	Amount	Description	Amount
Total		**Total**		**Total**	

$ SUN $ SEPTEMBER 27, 2020

Description	Amount
Total	

Notes

Weekly Expense Tracker

 MON SEPTEMBER 28, 2020

Description	Amount
Total	

 TUE SEPTEMBER 29, 2020

Description	Amount
Total	

WED SEPTEMBER 30, 2020

Description	Amount
Total	

THU OCTOBER 1, 2020

Description	Amount
Total	

FRI OCTOBER 2, 2020

Description	Amount
Total	

SAT OCTOBER 3, 2020

Description	Amount
Total	

SUN OCTOBER 4, 2020

Description	Amount
Total	

Notes

October 2020

Sunday	Monday	Tuesday	Wednesday
27	28	29	30
	Yom Kippur		
4	5	6	7
11	12	13	14
	Columbus Day		
18	19	20	21
25	26	27	28

Thursday	Friday	Saturday
1	2	3
8	9	10
15	16	17
22	23 Boss's Day	24 United Nations Day
29	30	31 Halloween

September 2020

Su	M	Tu	W	Th	F	Sa
		1	2	3	4	5
6	7	8	9	10	11	12
13	14	15	16	17	18	19
20	21	22	23	24	25	26
27	28	29	30			

November 2020

Su	M	Tu	W	Th	F	Sa
1	2	3	4	5	6	7
8	9	10	11	12	13	14
15	16	17	18	19	20	21
22	23	24	25	26	27	28
29	30					

Monthly Budget

Income		
Income 1		
Income 1		
Other Income		
Total Income		

Goal : _____

Budget : _____

Bill To Be Paid	Date Due	Amount	Paid	Note
			○	
			○	
			○	
			○	
			○	
			○	
			○	
			○	
			○	
			○	
			○	
			○	
			○	
			○	
			○	
			○	
			○	
			○	
			○	
			○	
			○	
			○	
			○	
Total				

Monthly Budget

Other Expenses	Date	Amount	Note
Total			

Total Income

Total Expenses

Difference

Notes

Weekly Expense Tracker

MON OCTOBER 5, 2020 **TUE** OCTOBER 6, 2020 **WED** OCTOBER 7, 2020

Description	Amount	Description	Amount	Description	Amount
Total		**Total**		**Total**	

 THU OCTOBER 8, 2020 **FRI** OCTOBER 9, 2020 **SAT** OCTOBER 10, 2020

Description	Amount	Description	Amount	Description	Amount
Total		**Total**		**Total**	

$ SUN $ OCTOBER 11, 2020

Description	Amount
Total	

Notes

_____
_____
_____
_____
_____
_____
_____
_____
_____
_____
_____
_____
_____

Weekly Expense Tracker

 MON OCTOBER 12, 2020   **TUE** OCTOBER 13, 2020 **WED** OCTOBER 14, 2020

Description	Amount	Description	Amount	Description	Amount
Total		Total		Total	

 THU OCTOBER 15, 2020   **FRI** OCTOBER 16, 2020   **SAT** OCTOBER 17, 2020

Description	Amount	Description	Amount	Description	Amount
Total		Total		Total	

SUN OCTOBER 18, 2020

Description	Amount
Total	

Notes

_____
_____
_____
_____
_____
_____
_____
_____
_____

Weekly Expense Tracker

MON OCTOBER 19, 2020

Description	Amount
Total	

TUE OCTOBER 20, 2020

Description	Amount
Total	

WED OCTOBER 21, 2020

Description	Amount
Total	

THU OCTOBER 22, 2020

Description	Amount
Total	

FRI OCTOBER 23, 2020

Description	Amount
Total	

SAT OCTOBER 24, 2020

Description	Amount
Total	

SUN OCTOBER 25, 2020

Description	Amount
Total	

Notes

Weekly Expense Tracker

MON OCTOBER 26, 2020   **TUE** OCTOBER 27, 2020   **WED** OCTOBER 28, 2020

Description	Amount	Description	Amount	Description	Amount
Total		Total		Total	

THU OCTOBER 29, 2020   **FRI** OCTOBER 30, 2020   **SAT** OCTOBER 31, 2020

Description	Amount	Description	Amount	Description	Amount
Total		Total		Total	

SUN NOVEMBER 1, 2020

Description	Amount
Total	

Notes

November 2020

Sunday	Monday	Tuesday	Wednesday
1 *Daylight Saving*	2	3	4
8	9	10	11 *Veterans Day*
15	16	17	18
22	23	24	25
29	30	1	2

Thursday	Friday	Saturday
5	6	7
12	13	14
19	20	21
26	27	28
Thanksgiving		
3	4	5

October 2020

Su	M	Tu	W	Th	F	Sa
				1	2	3
4	5	6	7	8	9	10
11	12	13	14	15	16	17
18	19	20	21	22	23	24
25	26	27	28	29	30	31

December 2020

Su	M	Tu	W	Th	F	Sa
		1	2	3	4	5
6	7	8	9	10	11	12
13	14	15	16	17	18	19
20	21	22	23	24	25	26
27	28	29	30	31		

Monthly Budget

Income		
Income 1		
Income 1		
Other Income		
Total Income		

Goal :

Budget :

Bill To Be Paid	Date Due	Amount	Paid	Note
			○	
			○	
			○	
			○	
			○	
			○	
			○	
			○	
			○	
			○	
			○	
			○	
			○	
			○	
			○	
			○	
			○	
			○	
			○	
			○	
			○	
			○	
			○	
Total				

Monthly Budget

Other Expenses	Date	Amount	Note
Total			

Total Income

Total Expenses

Difference

Notes

Weekly Expense Tracker

MON NOVEMBER 2, 2020			TUE NOVEMBER 3, 2020			WED NOVEMBER 4, 2020
Description	Amount		Description	Amount		Description	Amount
Total			Total			Total	

 NOVEMBER 5, 2020   NOVEMBER 6, 2020   NOVEMBER 7, 2020

THU Description	Amount		FRI Description	Amount		SAT Description	Amount
Total			Total			Total	

$ SUN $ NOVEMBER 8, 2020

Description	Amount
Total	

Notes

_____
_____
_____
_____
_____
_____
_____
_____
_____

Weekly Expense Tracker

 MON NOVEMBER 9, 2020   **TUE** NOVEMBER 10, 2020   **WED** NOVEMBER 11, 2020

Description	Amount
Total	

Description	Amount
Total	

Description	Amount
Total	

THU NOVEMBER 12, 2020   **FRI** NOVEMBER 13, 2020   **SAT** NOVEMBER 14, 2020

Description	Amount
Total	

Description	Amount
Total	

Description	Amount
Total	

SUN NOVEMBER 15, 2020

Description	Amount
Total	

Notes

Weekly Expense Tracker

 MON NOVEMBER 16, 2020   **TUE** NOVEMBER 17, 2020   **WED** NOVEMBER 18, 2020

Description	Amount	Description	Amount	Description	Amount
Total		Total		Total	

 THU NOVEMBER 19, 2020   **FRI** NOVEMBER 20, 2020   **SAT** NOVEMBER 21, 2020

Description	Amount	Description	Amount	Description	Amount
Total		Total		Total	

SUN NOVEMBER 22, 2020

Description	Amount
Total	

Notes

Weekly Expense Tracker

 MON   NOVEMBER 23, 2020   **TUE**   NOVEMBER 24, 2020   **WED**   NOVEMBER 25, 2020

Description	Amount		Description	Amount		Description	Amount
Total			**Total**			**Total**	

THU   NOVEMBER 26, 2020   **FRI**   NOVEMBER 27, 2020   **SAT**   NOVEMBER 28, 2020

Description	Amount		Description	Amount		Description	Amount
Total			**Total**			**Total**	

SUN   NOVEMBER 29, 2020

Description	Amount
Total	

Notes

_____
_____
_____
_____
_____
_____
_____
_____
_____

Weekly Expense Tracker

 MON   NOVEMBER 30, 2020   **TUE**   DECEMBER 1, 2020   **WED**   DECEMBER 2, 2020

Description	Amount	Description	Amount	Description	Amount
Total		**Total**		**Total**	

 THU   DECEMBER 3, 2020   **FRI**   DECEMBER 4, 2020   **SAT**   DECEMBER 5, 2020

Description	Amount	Description	Amount	Description	Amount
Total		**Total**		**Total**	

$ SUN $ DECEMBER 6, 2020

Description	Amount
Total	

Notes

_____

_____

_____

_____

_____

_____

_____

_____

_____

_____

_____

December 2020

Sunday	Monday	Tuesday	Wednesday
29	30	1	2
6	7	8	9
13	14 *Pearl Harbor*	15	16
20	21	22	23
27 *Dec. Solstice*	28	29	30

November 2020

Su	M	Tu	W	Th	F	Sa
1	2	3	4	5	6	7
8	9	10	11	12	13	14
15	16	17	18	19	20	21
22	23	24	25	26	27	28
29	30					

Thursday	Friday	Saturday
3	4	5
10	11	12
Hanukkah begins		
17	18	19
24	25	26
		Boxing Day (UK)
Christmas Eve	*Christmas Day*	*Kwanzaa begins*
31	1	2
New Year's Eve	*New Year's Day*	

January 2021

Su	M	Tu	W	Th	F	Sa
					1	2
3	4	5	6	7	8	9
10	11	12	13	14	15	16
17	18	19	20	21	22	23
24	25	26	27	28	29	30
31						

Monthly Budget

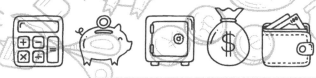

Income		
Income 1		
Income 1		
Other Income		
Total Income		

Goal :

Budget :

Bill To Be Paid	Date Due	Amount	Paid	Note
			○	
			○	
			○	
			○	
			○	
			○	
			○	
			○	
			○	
			○	
			○	
			○	
			○	
			○	
			○	
			○	
			○	
			○	
			○	
			○	
			○	
			○	
Total				

Monthly Budget

Other Expenses	Date	Amount	Note
Total			

Total Income

Total Expenses

Difference

Notes

Weekly Expense Tracker

 MON DECEMBER 7, 2020   **TUE** DECEMBER 8, 2020   **WED** DECEMBER 9, 2020

Description	Amount	Description	Amount	Description	Amount
Total		**Total**		**Total**	

 THU DECEMBER 10, 2020   **FRI** DECEMBER 11, 2020   **SAT** DECEMBER 12, 2020

Description	Amount	Description	Amount	Description	Amount
Total		**Total**		**Total**	

$ SUN $ DECEMBER 13, 2020

Description	Amount
Total	

Notes

_____
_____
_____
_____
_____
_____
_____
_____
_____
_____

Weekly Expense Tracker

 MON   DECEMBER 14, 2020   **TUE**   DECEMBER 15, 2020   **WED**   DECEMBER 16, 2020

Description	Amount		Description	Amount		Description	Amount
Total			**Total**			**Total**	

THU   DECEMBER 17, 2020   **FRI**   DECEMBER 18, 2020   **SAT**   DECEMBER 19, 2020

Description	Amount		Description	Amount		Description	Amount
Total			**Total**			**Total**	

SUN   DECEMBER 20, 2020

Description	Amount
Total	

Notes

Weekly Expense Tracker

MON DECEMBER 21, 2020

Description	Amount
Total	

TUE DECEMBER 22, 2020

Description	Amount
Total	

WED DECEMBER 23, 2020

Description	Amount
Total	

THU DECEMBER 24, 2020

Description	Amount
Total	

FRI DECEMBER 25, 2020

Description	Amount
Total	

SAT DECEMBER 26, 2020

Description	Amount
Total	

$ SUN $ DECEMBER 27, 2020

Description	Amount
Total	

Notes

Weekly Expense Tracker

 MON   DECEMBER 28, 2020   **TUE**   DECEMBER 29, 2020   **WED**   DECEMBER 30, 2020

Description	Amount	Description	Amount	Description	Amount
Total		**Total**		**Total**	

THU   DECEMBER 31, 2020   **FRI**   JANUARY 1, 2021   **SAT**   JANUARY 2, 2021

Description	Amount	Description	Amount	Description	Amount
Total		**Total**		**Total**	

SUN   JANUARY 3, 2021

Description	Amount
Total	

Notes

Made in the
USA
Columbia, SC